The Embrace

Song of the Soul

By Sharon L. Winnett

Energetic Therapy Publications

52
60
67
113
164
165

The Embrace

Song of the Soul

FIRST EDITION 2016
The Embrace, Song of the Soul

© 2014 by Sharon L. Winnett
Energetic Therapy Publications
Billings, MT 59102

Editor: Richard W. Gilson

Book design: Ambrose Taylor

ISBN: 9780978719333

Library of Congress Control Number: 2016913630

Printed by Lightning Source USA, UK, AUS

Contents

This secret Self in all beings is not apparent, but it is seen by means of the supreme reason, the subtle, by those who have the subtle vision.

Katha Upanishad

I hardly know how to express the depth of my gratitude for all the opportunities and lessons of my life. As always, I wish to thank my guides and loved ones who have been pivotal to my soul's growth. My family is a great treasure to me and my heart is full of gratitude.

Preface

The Embrace is a song from my soul that I sing with the world. As I celebrate any struggle in my daily life with the spirit of equanimity, I realize a freedom gained by a feeling of self-mastery. Daily reflection on my reactions and responses provides a vision of my soul's purpose and journey on this plane of existence. Gaining ease with all experiences, the great Work of self-realization unfolds. Planting the seeds of one's highest dreams each new day in an inner garden of potentiality and seeing it as our own increasing expression of self-love and inherent self-worth bears fruit deep within our being. Taking up our "work" in discovering our truth and path, as the manifesting principle of the Divine on earth and possessing all qualities the Divine love possesses, we seek only to realize this by surrendering to our Higher Self to guide us and by asking for the boldness to act according to this calling. Allowing this Truth principle to be our only guide, uplifting and inspiring us with each step, letting life flow through in our daily practice. Being unconcerned for the outcome, trusting it is certain we shall achieve our lofty goal. Being humble in our compassion, knowing we are an evolving soul.

It is my sincere hope that this work fills you with a sense of the preciousness of life and your process of discovery. I only long to share this sense of how cherished we are, how essential our voice to the world song. We are soul mirrors for one another, to peer into our truth. We enhance the collective experience. We may falsely judge our role as insignificant or hard to decipher, and the world's progress may seem obtuse and yet our Being is a fact and therefore must be enough. Our unique point of view and vibration is what is needed as we pursue joy, adding another glorious note to the symphony of life.

Created by Infinite Love and Mercy, I cannot believe we come to suffer but rather to celebrate and to embrace the lessons of our suffering as the growing edge of transformation into pure Joy. We come to explore and create. Nothing is asked of us but that we love ourselves and share this love with all creation. All is done more easily as we align our minds with the highest principles of Divine Love, have the modesty to know our limits and yet the courage to conquer them in every sphere of our life.

Child of God

Oh pure and open heart
Guide my life, my breath.
Let me fill the temple with roses, lilies and delicious fruit.
May I go to the alter bringing words that uplift and inspire.
The earth is our temple, our celebration of the Supreme.
For you my Beloved, my Life.
All that I am I place in your gentle strong hands.
You are my Mother and Father,
My brother, my guide.
May my days be my gift to you, who sent me forth.
To share love and laughter, tears and touch with all the world.
Please correct all error patterns in my mind.
May I send only the highest notes of love into our atmosphere.
Standing in a stream of unconditional love and light •
I join with all earth as I journey towards my inner light.
You are my playmate, my comforter.
To you I give all my being,
Let me remember Thee
As your blessed child.

Bow of Beauty

Oh, how I love thee Beauty.
Your silver jeweled bow
Aiming at my open heart,
Filling me with love.
Hummingbird knows the medicine we need
Gathering sweetness from the heart of Beauty, wherever she does roam
Proudly displaying rainbow colors, that pure nourishment can bring,
Ambrosia for the soul.
A flash of light she touches you
With magic fun and play.
This little warrior uplifts the world every day.
The rapid fire of her wings beyond what sight can bring,
To move with speed and ease
Small but mighty in her way.
Devoted flowers open to serve her need.
Perfume and color paint the world.
Her presence small and yet profound,
Reminds us of the innocence of love.
However small the act
The need for love is shared by all.
We take her gift, a sacred teaching
A rainbow feather, to see with Beauty's eye,
A sensual love, carried within deep chambers of each heart.
A union of rapture, a gift of romance,
Full of Joy abandoned unto Love
Shared lavishly with life.

Fountain of Youth

Massive creativity is held inside the atom,
We have seen its power to destroy.
The Sun offers to earth,
Its light to give life.
How we use our energy,
For love or fear,
Decides the effect we feel and experience,
By the intentions we hold dear.
We can create or split our molecules too,
Fretting over time yet not born,
Ethereal futures not manifest.
Let us drink instead from a Fountain of youth.
Within our powers of creativity
Dream all is possible,
Anything can occur.
Unleashing a powerhouse of passion
Calibrated with a plan of action,
A high intent and strong directed will.
We jump into the field to express, explore,
And to experience a rush of life, full tilt.

Hurts that Heal

We have been hurt
Our pain runs deep
How shall we heal?
A commitment of self-honoring.
Not going where we are not loved
Nor into places where we feel alone
Nor feeling trapped by forces from above
No power can infiltrate our peace.
Saying "no," to what feels uncomfortable
Yet taking risks, a leap of faith
Feeling the thrill of opportunity
Rising from the ash to say,
I have a voice and place on earth
My essence is of value, I am not
Dissuaded by judgement springing
From fear or doubt.
I will sing from the tallest tree,
High above, for all to see.
Shouting, "I am free."
Draw near to me my treasured friend,
Share the light
If love inclines us to,
Compassion and self-love
The key to heal any hurt we knew.

Goodwill

Consider the Source,
A universe made of Love
Every detail significant,
The structure of each cell
Filled with consciousness
Each particle alive.
Plants with their little veins,
Filled with lifeblood to sustain.
Animals know a natural harmony,
Taking only what they need.
Crystals buried deep hold a sacred frequency
Throbbing in the soil,
Building mountains' majesty.
Limitless variety, abundance in all forms
Desires forever reborn
A wondrous world the eye can see.
But higher still, Masters come
Upon the road, a path well worn
Every seeker does receive
Answers to his every need
And finds his Grace.
With trust, a Way
Is shown to us.
The fragrance of flowers gives
A message,
"All that is real is of Love."
We are the living truth of Beauty,
The essence of goodwill.
Be as we are
In innocence,
Unafraid of blossoming
Live in inner harmony and feel
A sublime experience of our own ideal.

Planting Seeds

Each day
A sacred opportunity
To plant the seeds of all my dreams.
All I seek flows down to me,
To help create the life I ~~seek.~~ *need.*
A body filled with light,
Not beyond but buried deep within this earthly plight.
A soil of peaceful inner sight.
A place of calm, where young and old alike
Dance in the sun, drinking crystal waters
To sustain all life.
I refuse to be fooled by what I do not like,
But crack the shell for the nut inside.
Nothing can prevent our awakening,
No effort is lost
No aliens of hidden fears shall pollute my dream,
I create a stronghold that is impenetrable.
I am the daughter of the King
Mother Nature's child,
Deserving the very best of life.
My meadows are filled
With sacred seeds.
Showers of love feed the streams abundantly
With every act, thought or deed
Joy springs eternally.
I live the life
God plans for me.

Contentment

No simple pleasure
Or high desire
No feverish pitch
Disturbs my sleep,
Trusting in the natural flow of things.
A way of life is found in this
Contentment in the little path,
The joy of the ordinary.
For looking closely at the details,
I find the universe blossoms innocently.
My own essence shining back.
Take our time, let things go by,
Absorbed in the miracle of life,
I find the wisdom of the spheres,
Entering my hungry ears.
The little song bird comes to say,
Have a happy joy-filled day.

Key of Understanding

We receive a golden key unlocking
Our Vital energy,
A key of understanding.
Revealing answers buried in a hidden cave,
Soothes and heals ones inner pain
A thread in a tapestry,
It gives us compassion for our neighbor's need.
Our psyche a river through which flows
The current of all we know.
We stand at the bank and consider its course
We see an infinite horizon
We wonder at its terrain,
Rocky places as yet untamed.
We long to climb its vista and see new sights.
This is a place we know and love
Here the Keys lie in wait.

Falling In Love

Holding our process in Its palm
Showing tender compassion
For the hurt we suffer from.
Taken beyond the boundary where reason may go
A world where the mind can hardly know
Feeling a place of peace at our core.
Trusting, we can not fail
We are held by the hands of Love.
In tender mercy we discover there
The power to truly heal the very root of fear.
Realizing why we came to be
We fall in Love
With our own humanity.

Forbidden Fruit

Tantalizing desire
Just beyond reach,
Greener pastures in which
To sink our feet.
A horizon disappearing from our sight
Gifts our neighbor seems to possess.
Love is rare because we love forbidden fruit.
If we join together
The sacred work begins,
Of cherishing each bright new day,
Unknown treats flow our way,
For these things we suffer so
Double-edged gifts,
For now we reap and then we sow.
What is the answer to our endless needs?
All the trinkets lay fallow at our feet.
If we find we can enjoy the ride,
We take these desires in our stride
See the thrill that dwells inside.
Our thirst quenched, rejoicing in the
Endless flow of life,
Savoring all perceived
Without attaching ourself to any particular form or need.
Giving freely we receive,
The treasure, at the core.
Eons spent discovering.
Desires the driving force of our wild steed
Who loves the joy of running free
To find the endless miracle,
Our state of mind that makes
It feel just like paradise.

Deep Love

Deep love cherishes and wants no more
Than no harm may ever darken our lover's door.
Every insult strikes the core,
A split is felt, a wound we can't endure.
Address the cause of any separation we feel.
Embrace one another as a gift of God,
Speak our truth with light and love
Honoring our equality.
Thanking them for their role
Revealing self-judgement's hold
From which we seek release.
As fear arises, up goes our guard,
Defending a brittle identity
A paper tiger that attempts to hide
A deeper understanding.
How do we learn to reconcile
Our longing for union
While defending a foolish pride?
Offering our little truths into the mix.
Seek freedom from our narrow mind
Our brother has come to shed the light.
Denial a brutal game, that will not be sustained
If love is to prevail.
Peace at all costs is false,
We must live by our virtue
Nothing worth sharing
If our fire is lost,
Our feelings both hearth and fuel.
Taking courage
Naked before our Destiny
Owning every tender place,
Finding a higher frequency
Honoring diversity is the way.
If love is not free it dies instantly.
Integrity and fair exchange,
Protecting a right to individuality.
The original Garden is found,
In innocence, we find deep love
A communal well-spring of brotherhood.

Witness Self

The watcher stands alert,
Sensing all the world.
Clear and bright the message comes.
Our highest self guides, step by step,
Perceiving patterns in endless forms.
Clouds passing in our minds
Transient beliefs, of unknown origin
Not who we truly are,
Yet we bring them here
To plant upon the earth.
The smallest things matter most
The root and seed, a flower or weed.
Feel the breeze, its song and tone.
Is it hot or is it cold
Answers that we seek,
Written on the gentle winds
Here is where we dwell.
Give full attention to the flow,
To know the season to reap or sow.
The fabric of the universe lives inside the self
Codes within our very cells
We may decipher our terrain
The wise course to proceed
By choosing love and harmony
With every aspect of our being.
Upon reflection, we may also surely find
Judgements always are the lie
Giving voice to our disharmony.
As the watcher we come to see
Beyond any fear we may perceive.
Inside and out, one and the same
Infinite patterns in the smallest things.
The Witness Self
Sits quietly and at ease,
A peace settles upon our mind
Behind the world we found so troubling.

Pearls of Wisdom

I am not sure how it is for you
In my life I have found
Seeking answers to who or what I am
A chasing for an endless pearl,
The nature of
Trials I may face
Fears that keep me in my place,
Ever searching for elusive peace
Circling the globe or seasons of a life
Feeding our senses on stories of old.
But is the answer in the hands of a sage
Does he have special access to Heaven's grace?
Or but a conduit for his own path,
Shining his light on what we too must face.
A fact that bears our scrutiny
Having access to infinite wisdom
The door must open for all equally
This shift changes the game
We see there is nothing to hide
All laid bare in the Mother's heart
Endless mirroring of all we hold
Revealing itself deep inside.
We have access to the Power and Strength
The Mother offers what we seek
Pushing its way to consciousness.
Willingness to ride the dragon's tail
We are carried home
Through the journey of our destiny.

Hidden Gifts

Every lesson
Has its gift.
It is the place
Where wisdom dwells,
A counterpoint
To Truth.
Eagerly embrace the wholeness
It now offers you.

Holding Presence

Holding Presence,
Bank the fire
Stoke the flame
Shielded by our love
Standing tall within.
The refrain must be
Hold the flame
This is the Way
A Brilliance
That is ours,
Shining everywhere
With everything.

Water's Way

Be as water flows
Allowing all.
Enter its stream
Trusting its power
Transforming and carrying all things.
Not offended by lowliness
Or ancient well
In which it may dwell
Nor pride in the loftiness
Of aglorious and mighty
Waterfall.
Never will it quell in its onward flow
Perfect vessel of non-resistance
It masters all.
We sit refreshed
Washed clean
And know this is our
Most cherished dream
Emulating Water's way
In all now we undertake.

Self-Giving

Divine Presence,
Love of the Absolute
What else is there to seek
Nothing else will really do.
For She is the font
Eternal refuge
Cleansing spring
The ever-present flowering
From which all life must spring.
Every breath is born again
To worlds yet beyond my sight
I see well enough
To understand
That I serve,
In little acts of kindness
To share and appreciate
Are gifts I possess
And so it is these I offer to the Absolute.

With Ease

Scent of a flower
Opulent and sweet
Your petals of velvet
Resting on a bed of green.
What an unexpected treat
This offering you give to me.
Your perfume fills my consciousness
With beautiful dreams
Soothing with great ease.

Gentle Breeze

Effortless we arise
Expanding into our lives.
Allowing the pulse and flow
Of the Divine to come.
Easily we can feel
The light of Love and inner harmony.
Soaring on a gentle breeze
No matter the tumult we may perceive.

Rose Scent

Why does Gardenia
Create her velvet flower
White and pure
Shining every hour?
From a core she draws upon
An opulent power.
Her intoxication fills the air
With good wishes everywhere.
The little Rose opens wide
Her petals fill her sky
With Love.
A soft perfume escapes her blouse
Filling my mind.
Perhaps cool Mint
Wears scalloped leaves
And refreshing green
To announce a cleansing nature
Or the stately Pine
Stands tall, a silent sentinel
A pungent protective shield
Adding his luminous essence
To purify and sanctify all life.
Eyebright and Chamomile
So calm and clear
Soothing the nerves that may jangle here.
Plants wear many shades and hues
Sweet or bitter we draw near
Directing and healing our weary minds
Bathing us in ethereal Light.
Their healing scents fill the atmosphere
Uplifting and inspiring us,
Restoring balance and harmony,
Sacred messages permeate our cells
Offering salvation from all alien
Fear-born spells.

Seat of the Soul

In a radiant glow
I find my Soul.
Here I rest
Tranquilly bedded.
A golden light so soft and bright,
A respite from the journey here.

Drawing deep from the inner core
Of Mother Earth,
Life sustaining vitality.
Fire of passion takes form
Giving birth of solid matter.
Inspiration flies into the winds
Rockets of becoming
Bursting forth from eternal Being.

Allow

If I will allow
All that is to be
The Peace of God
Is given me.

124

Space

Space defines my garden
Joy defines my space.
Here I plant my dreams
Living in eternal Grace.

Current's Flow

All aches and growing pains
Worries, fears of what yet may be
Are but little clouds,
Disturbances we create
How the world comes to be.
Masking our Essential Sun,
The ever placid and playful One
Has His way with us.
But always it is for the perpetual purpose of
True Joy, Peace and Infinite Love,
Revelling in a gradual return to our rightful home.
Unconcerned but Curious
Ever watchful in the Current's flow
Catching glints of Paradise,
The sparkling of the water's play
A fleeting instant
We sense so tenderly
Almost as a gentle breeze
The brush of a wing,
The mystical Heart of our Divinity.
Remaining forever whole and complete
Unblemished by a single day,
Knowing self-mastery is the only way.

Alignment

To Know
To See
To Feel
To experience Love
A stream of joy unending,
As resistance ebbs from consciousness.
Entering silently on great soaring wings,
I dive into an aqua pool,
For the catch I need.
Forgiveness cools my fiery mind
Tempered by the Sublime,
A rebirth occurs
As shadow disappears in light.
Washing from my inner memory
A dubious mind.
All finds its level and proper place
Balanced in the hands of Grace.
I am soothed and healed
My body returns to Source
Fully restored and lily white
I breathe deep
And sigh,
No more perfection is required.

Soul Joy

Reflected in a sacred pool
The inner Being
Comes shining through.
It speaks in tones just for you.
Bringing sweet delight
Telling of our inner might.
For in these quiet moments
We steal away
Reflecting only upon
Our Soul Joy
Each day.

Faire Light

Little lights
Who burn so bright.
Fill me with ethereal love
Carried on wings of rainbow light.
Harmonize my frequency
Body/Mind and Life,
With Mother so sublime
Gathered in Her arms
I am carried home.

In the Grove

Sit back
Relax
Let the good times flow.
No need to hurry
Or to hesitate
To taste each fruit fully.
If a hunch or inspiration
Comes our way
We may act without delay.
In the groove
We cannot miss
God has His ways.
Seeing every need
Met miraculously.

The Seeker

A man comes
To earth to see,
To look in the very
Heart of things.
Himself remembering
Places within his being
Where he buried
His golden rings,
Into sacred spaces
Filled with haloed graces
Knowledge of Ancient times,
Understandings of our fall and rise
So in some distant future age
He may return to seek again
Unlocking the door,
Ascending to a new glorious time
Of Heaven realized on earth again.

Mind Temple

In the sacred temple of the Mind
Where higher Reason reigns supreme
The gates are barred to thoughts unkind
For these are of the lower realms
And cannot here abide.
Here the ego has been tempered
And realized all it sought,
An essential drop in the Cosmic sea
Held inside the Supermind.
Here the air is pure and soft
The sanctuary with
a gentle peace
Soft colors permeate my being.
This is where I seek to dwell
And inspiration guides me well.
All righteous desires of my heart
Give courage of conviction
What is mine is realized
My temple filled with true Joy
And everlasting harmony.

Little Lights

Sweetest beings who uphold
Our natural world,
Mixing up the elements to bring
All the atmosphere of Mother Earth.
Who tend the trees and flowers
Who refresh the air and clean the streams.
Who stoke the fires in our hearts.
Their sacred work far exceeds their size
And if we call they will show us too,
The massive love we hold inside.
Permeating every cell with Spiritual light.
So make a place in the garden of the heart
And in the soil outside,
So these precious Little Lights
Will feel welcome,
To bless as they are wont to do.
To help mankind to feel the special gifts
They hold within.
To help us stand tall
No matter where the chips may fall.
To speak the truth we came to share
For we are here to make our mark,
To help the Ascension of our Earth.

Balance

The Soul hangs by a thread
Though not weak or unprepared,
Balanced exquisitely
All things in relation
With every other living being.

By Man's law
The scales tip to and fro
With heavy handed morality
Based on Ignorance and Fear,
A weight of lead
And perishable gold.
Endless moral codes bind his back
Forgetting his sublime heritage,
A righteous Brotherhood.
All born of One conscious source
Expressing the beauty of infinite diversity.

In higher frequencies
Spirit's Scale measures differently,
With a feather
So light and free.
Seeking, to my mind, inner harmony
Within our multiplicity.
Laying down of heaviness
Surrendering gently, over time,
To the knowledge all we truly need
Divine Love will provide.
To hold the Self in high regard
All life both great and small,
It is made by Universal Love.
Laughing and singing
For all we learn,
We touch our inner joy.

Sunlight

In Summertime
The shade is sought
Cooling the power of
Great sunlight.
By Fall we long
To receive the light of all we need.
And in the Winter
We turn to pray
Holding the Sun in our minds
Enveloping us each day.
With the return of Spring
We celebrate and run outside
To cast new seeds
Held throughout our long night.
A gentle Sun shines upon
Our innocence
And we flourish in His transforming Light.

Hands of Love

How painful it feels
This paradoxical scheme
Our human mind can not conceive
Much rhyme or reason to God's plan.
Exclusively we are focused to
The ever present loss and gain.
This Training flows to our core
A mantra of our faith and creed.
Seeing reality only in the physical realms
Without considering how things come to be.
Railing at the ever present flow
Longing for consistency.
A Life with ease
We struggle to conceive,
Or understanding how to receive
Every answer that we seek
All fulfillment of our Dreams,
Is in relaxation and let things be.
This living faith takes hold and the universe unfolds
Without the drama of our meddling.
Alignment with our Sacredness
Our Sublime purpose
Can be sensed only by
Surrendering into these Hands of Love.
Where the paradox yields the greater harmony within.
Our minds calm
Our spirit lifts
Full Gentle Power restored
Through our open imagining.
Sweet-natured children emerge again,
Our Being as creative engine of our worlds.

Praise

Man adopts a common stance
Which causes sorrow to my heart.
A peculiar quality of everyone's,
Insisting he is separate and matters not.
We may realize God is all
Creating in His mind,
Still insisting he stands alone.
Struggling to see the Artist's brush
Coloring the landscape with every thought,
Holding that God is good
But we are not.
What sort of madness is this
Tearing at his inner fabric?
Does not thought create the world,
The mighty oak holding its
Promise in a seed?
The essence of a mountain in a grain of sand.
And as we praise the little self for all it does
Do we not also honor Thee?

Blazing Brightly

Let no thought,
Word or deed
Diminish your right for
Blazing Brightly.
Do not slay the God within
By unkind words.
We bear a burden of exploring unknown lands
Poised on
The edge of the
Universal ledge
We are God's evolving world.
Mistakes are tools
In our belt
To test the theory of
Our greatness.
Buried beneath rock and soil
We must blaze a trail
Where none has gone before
So truly
We are not to blame
For any errors along the way
As innocence can not be
Our mighty travail.

I Have Come

I have come
Unto this time
To share, to love and to shine.
Without a care
For what the world thinks is real
They can not know what is yet to be.
I have come to be free
To cast aside what hinders me.
All past must finally also yield,
Until nothing constrains
My symphony.

Humble Garb

We enter the Stage
In Earth's presence.
We engage
Wearing such humble garb
No one knows
The Stellar Orb
Throbbing in our Heart.

Heavenly Light

Breathing in
Breathing out
I am filled with vibrant life
Ethereal love and heavenly light.
Sending out my deep gratitude
All are lifted to the greatest heights.
Round and round the circle spins
Joy abounds
Expanding fields within.
Cells vibrating to the Call
Radiant life answers all.
A beacon however small
Fills the atmosphere
As a living prayer.
Faeries bring the promise
I am waiting for,
Earth glowing, children sowing
Seeds of promise,
All God's blessings now restored.
I count these gifts unendingly
My frequency aligned with Thee.

We Matter

If I could send a message
To tell the precious children
Our worth is seen
In spite of circumstances,
That may refuse to yield.
Hold onto even the smallest thread,
A fleeting dream
A moment in time,
When there was peace
A sense of light.
Build upon this
However vague.
Trust you have all it takes
Stand tall and thrive
Never yield to tempting fears
You can not fail in God's eyes.
Be kind to the sensitivities of your inner child,
Awaken each day and take your hand
Nurture every dream you have.
Regardless of pain we feel
We have come to set the world free.
Old habits die hard, it has been said,
So patience is our dearest friend.
We must not settle for false reprieves
Or drown our sorrows in petty things.
Approval can not be given from without.
Others come to test our resolve,
Am I being true to me?
Above all else I would say
We carry a new and sacred seed
Revealing to the world
What real Love can be.
Not conventions worn and dull
Or on a holiday where we hate to go,
But deep abiding Grace
Of holding Love in every space.
To face ones demons I know a truth
We are precious by our very courage
To laugh at fear.

Magic Formula

What is it
A miracle worker does?
Is it a crystal, bell or unction,
Or their intention of Divine Love?
Two elements weave the cure
Intention and flame of Faith.
A magic Formula
Where healing may occur.
A frequency inside
High and sweet
Resonating from every cell
Restores heavenly sight
From above we see the light,
A dynamic state, a cup-sharing place,
Standing side by side before the Creative Force.
Healing is complete instantly
The remedy has been received
According to the truth of every need.

Christ Child

Little child pure and sweet
Snow white and glistening.
Listening quietly,
Her wisdom speaks, guiding me
Where all doubt is but a passing breeze.

Poise

I move with poise
The Guardian of my spirit
Whose loving energy
Is guiding me.

Instinctual Wisdom

There is a seed
Buried deep within,
Engine of all creativity.
An emotional guidance system
Fueling our dreams,
Carries us to the Moon
And back again.
We check the weather
To prepare,
Let us check the inner systems
For repair.
See what our mind
Has been conjuring.
Aligning instead with the
Instinctual Wisdom
Each possess.

Power of Love

What can we not achieve
With the power of Love
We do receive,
Guiding the flow of everything
Towards Joy and Peace.

Harmony

Witness the passing of each day,
All events that come our way.
Little bumps of discontent
Tiny signals of our unrest.
Heed their warnings of distress,
Breathe slowly,
Feel its healing rhythm
Taking in more than air,
A vital restoration of the ethers
Enter to repair.
Gently soothing, settling down
Patterns of harmony are found.
Adjust our speed
Aligning gears, a balancing resonance
Of our Soul.
As water flowing easily over rock and shell
Moving energy easily back and forth.
No resistance, no judgements found,
All push or pull in the flow of life
Intended only to energize.
We may proceed with ease and grace,
Here insights appear
In time and space.

Symbols

Ancient keys reveal
Doors to our Subconsciousness
A storehouse of opportunity to our most
Precious gifts.
A soul's library throughout the ages
Comes here to rest,
Beyond thought
Word or deed
An ancient language.
Through ethers vibrations emanate
Color, sound and harmony
Simple yet so profound.
Mind catches sparkling reflections
Of these treasures held
Repeating patterns
Rhythms from unseen wells
Reminding us of lessons learned.
Untold gifts come beckoning
By every inspiration felt
Unlocking a knowing
From hidden mystery
Innate understanding of the world we perceive.

Lovers

Entwined in an endless embrace,
Loving of all our Creator makes.
Reclining easily in time and space
Upon a hammock of gossamer threads.
Innocent of what we may not see.
Beyond horizons of eternity
Truth shall be revealed
We name her Synchronicity.
Dancing under a starry night
To realize we are one with life.
Enter Ecstasy of God's delight,
A dream of our true reality.

Calling Down the Heavens

Invocation is made
Commanding heavens to descend.
Heart open wide,
Our persistent call is heard
We seek to enjoy blessings of only Light.
Staking our claim
Upon this land,
Fulfillment of promises long held
To realize our inherent worth,
And it is this that saves our earth.

Heaven in Every Cell

Planting seeds
Our held belief
Let Nature work Her Way.
Penetrating our consciousness today
Heaven enters every cell
There to reveal
Spirit working throughout life.
Light pours out where vision
Has been restored,
Blossoming where healing occurs.
Not limited by our Achilles' heel
Behind the weakness a sacred power is revealed
Infinite capacity
To create
Ever born anew in time and space.

Duty

What can be added
Or subtracted from Divinity?
Is the flower sufficient
Seeking light to thrive
Or feel a need to belittle itself
For its appointed place in life?
Does it bloom where its planted
Without a care for the soil wanting there?
Man too is Nature bound
While in a mortal sheath
His blood and bones a simple vehicle,
Subjected to these laws of carbon life.
Yet he feels fear about his plight.
His dilemma of action in
Choosing to see the Light.
Ever his quest unfolds
To realize his destiny.
Troubled by his choices
Between the dark and light.
He must reclaim his faith
And birthright,
Dwelling securely forever in God's own mind
Lacking nothing
He is guided by the Light.
His only task is to persist
For Truth is absolute.
In our hearts a note rings clear
We are innocent and pure.
Our duty seems to be to see this here.
By His very name no error may occur
Existing in Grace
For all eternity.

If...

If I am in God
Of God, by God
I must be very holy.
Perhaps not quite a finished piece
But still the bones must be sound,
And I too must be in all I see
In the table and the mountain
In rock and in sea, the
Also in the Heavenly
Stars that shine so high above me.
I can not even be too upset
If I am bound
To all I see,
If I may also love every permutation
Of my Divinity.

Chalice

Pouring Essence
Into forms
A Holy vessel for God's joy.
The spark of the creator
Enters here.
Our atoms are whole
Even if the mind is split
Self-expression seems to need various perspectives
In which to see.
Contrast provides the mirror
Through differences
Where the non-physical can discover Himself
The vast within the particular.

Throughout history we clearly see
Man senses his divinity,
He tries to make it a power outside
To grasp his meaning.
In the end the call sounds
Take up our will, however small it feels,
Acknowledge there must be a Light of Life
A consciousness answering a greater call.
Into this Chalice,
Body and identity harmonize
Designed to serve,
And share our blessings
With all the world.

More Light

Offered endless opportunity
To test our strength,
There comes a day
When tests fall away.
Joining with the Master
We align
Calling only for more light eternally.
For purity and calm
Equanimity in facing every storm.
The virtue of the challenge is understood,
To strengthen our resolve.
Rising into Mercy's ethereal realm
Gratitude is felt.
Safely at Heaven's gate,
We realize our destiny.

Grievances

Let my sight
Come to me
Piercing Grievance's
Iron grip.
Tearing fine threads of my being
Seeking revenge for slights I perceive.
Refusing to hold these thoughts as real
And look instead to Truth.
A miracle mind-set
Of our shared Christ consciousness.
Come save me from my withering beliefs
Change my mind,
Free me from petty arguing
To find the calm I seek.
Restore to me my innocence,
My inheritance
My Birthright,
Of inner peace and harmony,
Of Infinite Joy
So I may see the face of Love
Shining now in me.

Soldier On

Trudging on earnestly,
Compassion brings nourishment
Reaching out to embrace
Each form in life,
Reflecting rich images to our minds
Revealing our Soul's desire.
Don't give in or up
Though there will still be trials,
A Power great lies hidden
Working out our lives.
We brush it lightly in times of peace
Encouraging sublime retreat.
As inheritors of potential Grace
Chin held high
Dearest brother and I
Becoming Masters of all life.
Tomorrow is a new and better day
In this we can rely.
Understanding builds a framework,
Step by step the Soul does lay
A path from which we can not stray.
Perhaps grim earnestness
Must pave the way
Strength learned every day
Judgements cast aside
Even hasty retreats may be self-honoring.
It matters not what others say
They play perfectly their role,
Helping us to reach the light
By triggering a response,
Deep emotions driving me
So I might gain self-mastery.
Earth is for the brave at heart,
A place to heal suffering
Slay dragons of ignorance
By embracing all with Mercy's ear.
Shooting for lofty heights
Aim high
Each in his own sacred way
To catch the moon.

Healing Command

That every cell, fiber,
Aspect of my being
Be filled
By the all-pervasive gentle
Light of Grace.
Permeating my atmosphere
With harmony
My dear body does most appreciate,
An easy mind
Full of wonderful joy
My heart bursting with song.
Transporting me down the road of life
Carrying only my heart of love,
Sharing with everything
Both seen and unseen,
For in me lives a bridge of Faith.

Ease

Born in Fire
Feeling great need,
A compelling force
We all perceive.
Struggling to redeem
The hidden life-force energy.
Our sight is focused narrowly,
Right and wrong, dark and light,
A tragic split we feel inside.
Prayers flow out to hidden realms,
Instinctively we sense potential yet unborn.
In a world of unexpected incidents,
Intentions set we soldier on
Relinquishing control
The little will insufficient
Tender shoulders grow sore.

Transformational Energy
Unlimited Power takes up the cause.
Our greatest Nemesis
We must learn to rule the mind
Make our sincere offering,
Every deed paves our way,
Work reigns supreme on this plane,
But in letting go
We ease our greatest chore.

Redemption

I learn to see
All that I perceive
As sent by a True Self,
Clearing my vision of erroneous beliefs
Revealing progressively
The Golden One who dwells in me.
Within the glow of this heavenly light
All my errors are set right
Every step aimed to bring to me
The righteous desires of my highest Self.
Sacred opportunities to grow in strength
Developing a vast unshakable Faith
To know the God in me,
Unlimited and completely free.
Beneath each grievance
Shines my Love,
The Well-Spring we all drink from.
Looking deep into the face of strife
I see my judgment, made in haste,
Placed lovingly for my liberation.
Now I celebrate,
The freedom it has given me
Redemption from all fear.

My Sun

My body is strong
Fed by Infinite Love,
I align with this strength,
My Sun
Filled with Power
Of Holy Grace.

Sinless

No judgment has been levelled
To affect innocence,
No fear can be warranted
To eternal beings.
We can not judge if we can not see
Infinite possibility.
So here we may rest and know
True ease.

Contentment

Thank you for
This pretty place
Reminding us of healing Grace
It feels like our heavenly home
Contentment's breeze fills my lungs
A place where we may come
And share our love.

The Cause

Taking up our Cause
A natural inclination
The Prime Directive
Buried in our DNA,
By some subtle code we came to play.
From this God-cell energy
We look out into the world to see
The Face of our own Divinity
The Christ child
The son of God,
We have been promised, is our
Birthright and true home.
In every living thing
This truth must surely be,
For we are not separate from our Source,
If God is All as he must be.
Knowing this we are transformed.
Through all mercy, we are restored.

Large or Small

Size is irrelevant
It matters not
Anything is soil
Into which we plant
The seeds of our own destiny
For the mastery that we seek.
All matters large or small
Reveal our journey,
Of what our soul intends.
But to call out to the highest light
For protection
Strength, guidance and for love,
To so purify our offering
The path is smoothed
And our promised world
Comes into view,
Where no more tests
Will be necessary.
For this alone
We welcome every little opportunity
To betake of our just deserts.

Our Shining Light

I am not responsible
For all that you may feel
This is a personal domain
From which we may not stray.
Equal in capacity
And unique in our response
Each of us a special mirror
For the viewing of our soul.
Neither may I judge
What I may behold
For hidden in the core
A treasure to be found.
Still I send out energy
That is corrosive to my love
I may be certain
I will suffer greatly
And the mirror will reflect
The judgement of my inner self
Shining clearly back to me.
This is the greatest gift
A treasure which is hard to hold
But to see in clear relief
A bias hidden deep within
Finally revealed
Gives me new power
To master my own destiny.
To choose to share forgiveness
With great humility.
To honor ever more
Our shining light
That we all share
And let this be the image in my mirror.

Frequency

Behind all Love
We feel here
Source gives unlimited supply.
We open to receive these gifts
Filled with joyful harmony
Sharing our love endlessly
This frequency reflecting Divinity.

Deep Garden

We wear a social face,
A constricted mask
Taken on by our social training
And our own world view.

Out of fear we will be cast aside
We pull our punches
Resentful and pinched from life,
To suffer with a painful lie
Imposing our distress on others' lives.
Hoping if we can share this prison
In which we now reside
Our loneliness and suffering will decline.
Secretly longing to speak our mind,
Yearning to be seen, to matter
Breaks the shackles of our mind
Pulls out the stops eventually
To risk all fear and fly.
Realizing this sacred place
A deep garden where our truth resides,
Freely breathe new vital energy
The thrill of life courses through our system
Tapping this hidden storehouse of creativity,
Tasting even one drop of this ambrosia
Restorative and fulfilling,
Causes a thirst that must be quenched.
No longer can we abide restriction in our stride,
Unwilling to hide
Accessing Power's source
Our everlasting eternal youth.
A conscious collaborator of our world
Our atoms fill with light
And gratefully we sing
Without design
And share our precious voice
With all the earth.

Nevermore

To walk alone
Nevermore
No dark night
So far from shore
My friend and comrade
Sharing now my joy
Dwelling in my bosom fair
Flowing out everywhere,
For here Peace comes to rest
Sun shines without a care.

Spirit of the Wind

Laying down my sword
Of righteousness,
I receive my shield instead.
Spirit of the Wind
Offers conviction as She yields
Truth the only weapon needed.
Honesty and courage walk by my side,
Teaching me to be kind,
Forgiving every insult I hold inside.
Remembering all is made by Love,
My brothers come to help me heal
To encourage me,
Until all within is revealed.

The Will

Dear sweet Mother/Father
Who created me,
I am
As you would have me be.
Your time unfolds perfectly.
Bold and brave I step
Knowing there can be no rush,
Soothing my inner fright I carry on
This great work, my destiny.
Completion is at hand,
Who knows when realization may dawn
As great bells peal,
Sound upon great sound
Reverberating throughout the land.
The fire flames high,
A great pillar of golden light
As a beacon within every man.
Miracles abound.
Now is the time,
Today is the day!
My sole refrain,
I am whole and complete in every way.
Effortless as I release the reins,
A gentle nudge shows the way,
I bow in deepest gratitude
One mind, One Self
Aligning gradually
I walk with growing confidence
That your Will
Knows the way.

Humble

Humble enough
To let the Work
Proceed in me undisturbed.
To receive all gifts,
Allowing life
To flow through as a guiding light.
I offer thanks and soldier on,
With a cheerful face
Based in loving Grace.
Shown with every step
My true Identity
I grow in faith.
A great Star above,
My Guardian and guide,
Shines upon me all the day.
And buried deep within my soul
I come to see my choice.
One with my Divinity
Not fending on my own,
Or in a random universe unknown.
But held close in the Mother's arms,
Cherished as her sacred child.
God within my very bones,
Chose an ultimate experience
Of liberty.

Many Faces

Every lesson
Brings its gift,
A greater understanding
Replacing fear with faith
Offering to us
That Truth is infinite
Not narrowly confined,
Wearing many faces to illuminate,
There is no other way of it
Diversity is our guide.
What lies beneath is unity
Holding all in Light.
For this we come
With great purpose
To celebrate
This wisdom growing in our soul.

Source Energy

Whatever feels good to me,
Aligns with my Source energy.
God is not outside somewhere,
Judging us from some remote location
But dwells in every single cell,
Our inner lover guiding us.
The thrill I feel in finding
Where my passion dwells
The Inner body so alive
A subtle field of pulsing energy.
Even in deepest pain one may find
Sweet soft refrain.
A peace that holds us gently,
Gives us hope and strength
With courage we live and thrive
Touching this sacred place,
We sense at once a force propelling us,
New doors opening at every step,
Carrying the mantle of our life
Pushing gently from behind
To leap into the great unknown.

Divine Messenger

I've heard that there was a time
Before the animals ruled,
Our Earth was covered in flowers.
Such a lovely picture conjured in my mind
So gentle and sublime,
Many colors and fragrance sweet
Such a peaceful place to be.
Imagine the innocence
To enter here
Softening our repose
Resistance melting in the Sun,
Surely the Eden of old.
What if we could reclaim this age
This innocence into which we are born
To see the ancient message.
All the flowers help
In the remembering.

Every Turn

Equality of spirit
In the throes of change
Even the depths of turmoil.
Calm waters may return
By our choosing Grace and harmony
In every step we take.
Picking up the pieces
Gathering the fallen blessings
Holding them close to the breast
Stepping forward
Walking on
With courage and with strength
With fearless faith
At every turn.

Fountain of Love

Wash me
Eternal fountain of Love.
Fill me,
Every cell
With glorious light from above
Absorbing its life giving energy
To capacity,
Overflowing out into the world
And beyond
Onwards into infinity,
Blessing me
Blessing thee
Blessing land and sea
For all eternally.

Divine Goodness

Our greatest gift
That I can see
Is realizing our divinity.
All that's holy
Sweet and good
Reflecting back to God
The true value of our daily offering.
Divine Goodness as we may conceive
To all we see,
We hold within
This sacred seed
However simple it may now seem.

Living Prayer

A mantra on the go
A way for life to flow
As is our need
Progressive tendencies
New perspectives
All here is provided for.
Trusting each step we take
No matter the risk
So innately unique and still
Each connecting to the whole.
Compassion reveals our essential link
To every living soul.

Full Potential

Refreshing breeze
The ground is cool
Puddles shimmer yellow-gold
Prismatic dew adorns the soil
Little rainbow treasure chest.
Tiny seeds plant themselves
Snuggle into softened soil
Knowing as ice does melt
They shall celebrate by flowering.
Winter Sun shines ever bright
Even tho' we turn aside
To ponder now our inner life.
Air is crystal blue
We are refreshed by her mist
Stars shine fiercely bright
I swear that they come closer too,
Perhaps it is the winter night
That makes them dip so low.
Strategically, we plant our dreams
So as the thaw grows we too
May be born anew.
Protected by the Mother of all
Until our vision grows strong and clear
Our full potential realized
A paradise on earth revealed.

Sufferings End

The book is written
To the end
Experience teaches step by step.
We may not know what lies around each bend
But still
We must arrive
At long last
To Suffering's End.
So stay awhile,
Why hurry here
Laugh in life
The journey need not be so filled with strife.
Use time as a treasured friend.
Dust our feathers,
Preen and bathe with joy
All are taking flight
From whence we came.
Ascending to the mountain peaks
Towards an endless plane
Knocking now on Heaven's gate,
No space for fear or pain.
Our work is great
In opening to Grace
Letting heaven permeate
Every atom of this plane.

Golden One

In my mind's eye
A steady course
By keeping the Golden One
Center stage.
Looking up
I hold my faith,
Soaring into the universe.
Tho' I may not really know what lies ahead
Somewhere within
A core abides guiding by the felt sense I have,
Whenever I express
The love I hold inside.
I know I must be made very strong
So no gale can shake my inner root
Or weaken my resolve.
I know I must be reunited
With my Truth,
For even in this shadow land
The Sun does shine upon my face
Each day without any effort on my part.
So I may conclude all is born of Grace
This too must be Heaven's place
And we can not really stray from home.

Transcendence

I stake my claim
To what is mine
A pioneer in a land of time
Endeavoring to hold my ground
To aspire to transcendent Truth
To gather my nature into a unified whole.
I can not fathom the greater game
But know that Love is my foundation stone
And if I can see
The Love in every living being
Each expression of life
Then I am on my way
To my promised land.
As I perceive
A single aim,
All on this earth joins
An evolutionary game
To thrive and grow,
To feel the peace it brings to every soul.
Pain is a resistant edge
A hardened place I fear to tread
Believing I must defend my plight
Some valiant struggle
In darkest night.
Consider how to find release
Relief from all disharmony.
As the Sun must surely rise
I come to see, it is the narrow
I must discard,
Surrendering to a gentle ease.
Even this my mind can't quite conceive
Attaching value to the pain of life.
But these doubts too are set aside.
My Being has designed a destiny,
Without regards to Time,
To stand within my Well-Spring
To see my true Nature.
Renewed I travel on,
Until no more lessons need be learned.

Natural Flow

Walking the path
Instinct leads *an*
Noticing a rhythm to things,
Expanding and contracting
We breathe.
To veer from this allowing
With even the smallest thought
Constricting pain overwhelms
Rapid shrinking of ~~our being~~. *my heart.*
Nature teaches so patiently,
Her infinite wisdom of organic flowering
Mother tends her garden well.
Never hurrying or out of step, she spins her web
Reeling in her circle dance.
She fills our air with flowery perfumes
To uplift, to sooth,
With endless Beauty of her loving heart.
We are of the Elements
Our hearts full of ocean's depth,
Fiery creature Desire ignites our visions
An earthly body bears the sweetest fruit,
Reveling in sensual pleasures.
Gentle breezes caress our face,
Warm encouragement and strength with each new dawn
A constancy in our shining sun,
The great symbol of Power and Unity
And love for everyone. *the*
Moon's many gentle faces shows us the kindness of Grace*s* .
A disciplined mind lifts us to our highest joy
As wings of air,
We soar with eagles
Set free, envisioning
New worlds as yet unseen.
Communally we satisfy our need for deep exchange
As Brothers
Working together to make the lift,
Witnessing the natural flow
And emulating Nature's way.

Gathering

Our senses
Our gifts
Our offerings
Our love.
All Strength
And Faith
We gather all
To assist us in
This life we live.

Arising

We are rising
Each and everyone.
Arising
Each time we choose love.
Gathering the Ascended Ones
Angelic and Celestial realms
Pulling together by our prayers
Great threads
Woven in the story of our time.
Surrendering all
To Transcendent Truth
Letting go a little more every day
Trusting we can not fail,
Rebirth we seek
Remembering our common
Divinity.

Golden Key

What do we seek
Above all else?
What is the cure
For all ill-health
What remedy for wars and discontent?
To me Compassion
Is the Golden Key,
The only lasting remedy.

To know the fear we hold within
Is universal for all our kin,
Perhaps even of our
True beauty within.
Emotions fill the atmosphere
Guns shatter the peace we build
Birds flee, flowers swoon
Waters acidify in impending gloom.
We feel attacked
Survival mechanisms
Poison our mind
Striking out or in holding back
We resist the sacred offering.
Compassion sees only Love
Our deepest need to feel as one
With understanding
We widen
We breathe
With our best intentions,
We fly free.

House of Joy

I will build a House of Joy
A place for fun
For me and everyone.
Filled with laughter
Love and play
Gardens of flowers
Where we may dance every day.

Prism

Poppy turns her head to see
Ever Bright,
We follow her steadfast gaze
To behold also a golden light.
Our Mother's arms held wide
In her embrace we live and thrive.
A sea of blue tranquility
Absorbed within Her healing strength
She gives us courage
To carry out our tasks.

Perfumes of Love
She imbues
Flowers of a thousand names
Reminding earth of Spirit's
Everlasting bloom.
Compelled too are we
To seek Her Light
To see the glistening prism
Of all life.

Cruel World

What can we do
When our world feels cruel
How can a brother hurt another
When we are as God created us,
What can be the point of endless suffering?
To Pivot our thoughts,
Such firm beliefs
And realize everyone is there to teach.
Our judgement
Blinds and binds us tight,
Hiding the sweet innocence
We hold inside.
Shutting down
We retreat
For danger lurks
Beneath our feet
We dare not expand or seek to understand.
We share a common brotherhood,
Finding strength
And common ground
A cord connecting heart and mind.
Offering of compassion
For shared fears
We find we hold the love we seek.
And understand the joy our cruelty
Longed to teach.

Inner Strength

It may seem
a curious truth
That in our weakness
We find our strength,
Hidden under its heavy cloak.

Pushed
Against a wall
Sharp contrast goads us.
Pivoting
Into new fields of truth
Seeking harmony
New patterns set.
No wish to tarry
In this place of pain
We strike out
For some unknown land
With new resolve
To celebrate our new-found place
Nor doubt our worth again,
Purified by the fire of
Inner Strength.

Quest

The endless quest
A daily search
For Transcendent Truth,
Truth that can not be undone
By any division under our Sun.
Higher and higher we climb
Never certain who is our guide.
Building faith in darkest night
Trusting we must surely reach the Light.
Deep blue fires
Pour down from beyond
To give us strength.
Persistent desire
Pushes to reach the light.
Amplifying core beliefs
We decipher
A higher cause within all things.
Pioneering a path
None have gone just this way,
Yet some secret mission
Seems well underway.
Step by step
Recognizing signs
Envisioning how life could truly be.
Winds may still howl
Pain within may roar
We must calm and rule the mind
Establish inner harmony.
And if we chance upon a place
Where peace prevails
All our needs
Provided for
And hear the voice of gentle Grace,
Our quest was not in vain.

Comparisons

An odious quality,
A game of mind
Lain upon each child.
The never ending play,
Designed to darkly entertain
And hide a terror held inside.
In every comparison hides a forgetfulness
How similar we truly are,
The single heart of God
That lives in us.

False judgement
Selects between
Some transient right or wrong,
As if it held a moral certitude.
Our limiting view focuses
On the surface of a personal truth
A shifting landscape.
The eternal awakening within the Universe
From which springs this strange and varied world.
Behind all things we sense
A greater Truth we cannot touch.

Looking for our common thread
Focused on what we share instead
We find a new world blossoming.
Each comparison
Leading to a new vista
An ever more inclusive view.
We expand and feel release
A new progressive state of mind.

The Best

Intentions, our most potent and handy tool
An arrow focused at the Moon.
Seeking all that we wish were true
Focuses and trains the mind
To look for hidden treasures
In all it finds.
To act in ways to support our highest hopes
An imagined bliss all may enjoy,
The best we can conceive at any given time.
To perceive as well
A natural limit in our ability,
The future then may be released
Into the hands of our Divinity,
A power that takes up our acts and prayers.
And we may rest
Assured
For we have chosen to see the best
To trust the limitless power of our intent.
Our destiny is forged.

Father's Table

I come to dine
At my Father's table.
A banquet has been set,
Every good food is made
With love and harmony to my taste.
We may drink our fill and be content
Without a care,
Nourished by the Infinite.

Smile at our Destiny

Dear Teacher may
Your words inspire,
Bring forth the growth.
The traveler needs
To hold onto Joy,
To trace His steps,
Ascending on a spiral path
From the outer world
Into his core and back again,
That he may rejoice
In endless cycles of Infinity,
And smile at his destiny.

The Open Door

Make the command,
Take a stand,
No need to hesitate
We come equipped
Fully capable to make the trip.
Knock on the door
With great resolve.
Await beyond any doubt
For it will open
Without unnecessary delay.
Every little miracle
That comes our way
Opens now a sacred gate.
We may step into a Paradise.

Aspiration

Attention to detail
In the flow
The field in which we thrive,
Planting seeds
Of aspiration
Beyond our wildest dreams
Where pigs do fly.

Mother Divine

My fervent prayer
The time at last,
All ancient promises
Have come to pass.
For all your children
Of this earth,
Oh, sweet Mother
Let it be we are filled with Grace.
We return fully without delay
We remember our precious Divinity,
Harmonized and filled
With strength
Of our Love
Of the joy in celebrating
Life on Earth,
For it is here and nowhere else
We are transformed.

164

No Regret

What is the value
Of our mistakes
The purpose regret
Does make?
If we had travelled this way before,
Had some premonition
Of a path unknown
Never willingly would we
Enter our potential doom.

Surmising now
After all,
We come to realize
What feels right.
What leads to love
And Innocence.
We may lament our former ignorance
Still we celebrate its gift to us
As we arise to see a vista
Grown rich and wide.

Pleasure Principle

To realize we are made of God
Is the heady fuel
Which drives us on.
Ruling our atoms
Encoded in our conscious cells
Dwells a spark of the Ineffable!
We question how we sense this Truth
Our little mind knows not the way,
Ancients point to a deeper path
Intuiting a hidden Focal point,
We barely fathom the heart of it.
A burning question rears her head,
Well if this is so
How do we pierce this veil?
What is my truth
Where shall I turn, whatever shall I do?
Epiphany longs to reveal
Our value and inherent worth
A radiance of which all Teachers speak,
This Becoming we call our Self.
How does the Being shine with every breath
A witness of the expanding universe,
When barely we conceive
The ground beneath our feet?
Forced to tend instead to each small thing
Every event in which we act as king.
The Infinite squeezed into finite shapes,
Imagining he may fully animate
With all Powers at His command
To create a Heaven upon our land.
A Supreme Pleasure Principle
Of Pure Love
Opening all doors
A compelling enthusiasm with every breath
Spurs us forth
To celebrate, to share, to grow
The great work we all share.
We come to know ourself.

Love

Filtering down from above
Heavenly rays
Fill us with great joy
In the common everyday
All little things
That come our way
Adding to the Mystery
Something precious that truly heals
Here we call it
Love.

Gratitude

My gentle heart
Finds its shield
Impenetrable to any sword,
Inside the light of Gratitude.
Here I feel at One
With all love
Life and brotherhood.
Here I see a way
For Beauty expressed
Each and every day.
A prayer goes out
For all I care about
Surrender finds its place
For here I find I am safe.

Surrender

White flag of surrender
But not of defeat
Instead to a Power
Well above my own clay feet.
A place where one may feel truly free
May finally breathe,
Letting go
To all we see
Trusting in our own
Hidden Divinity.

Earth's Wonders

Seeking the Divine
In every stream and flower
In the breeze
The land, the trees,
The faces of my brother
Earth's endless wonder,
Finding Love in everything.
As I while away the hours
Dive deep into my industry
Love is also finding me,
My self-knowledge flowers
Joining increasingly
Into everlasting harmony
No storm can shake from me.

As I Am Healed

Traversing life
Meeting all
Who understand my plight,
Deep longings
Desire to share
My inner language understood there.
Fear's shadow serves to quicken me
Towards my inner sanctuary.

In my small corner of the world
I strive to fully realize
All connections
In my internal tapestry
Every effort that I make
Each sweet breath I take
I am healed.

This energy spills out from me
Back into all the world I see,
Rejoicing and expanding
Affecting every plant and stone
The very atmosphere
Of my dear home.
All this makes me glad
Beyond imagining.

Mind the Gap

The little space
Between where we stand
And wish to be
Lies pain
Waiting quietly.
Mind the gap
It is only a stretch between
This place and that.
Fly free
Let all things be.

Power Down

Lights out
Power down
Just a hint,
To be sure.
Feel the return
To Innocence,
Knowing and seeing
Without the mind
To obfuscate.
Enter briefly a silent Sublime.
Nature comes into our home
Provides her rhythms,
Sun still shines
Or we are cast into the night
Scurrying to find
A candle light.
We take a moment
With little else to occupy our time
With Power off
We are subdued
Gaze upon
The storm outside
And find ourself renewed.

Light Vessel

Oh to be a vessel
Filled with light,
Golden Grace
To fill my mind
Not a speck of darkness left
No doubt nor strain
Or any Ignorance.
From this great and lofty place,
Mind surrenders momentarily,
The Immensity of Unity humbling
Like looking into outer space.
Filled with Joy
Everything in its True and Proper place.
Everyone and everything
I might behold
Flourishing and feeling whole
This everlasting Peace,
Seems the only worthy place
Now to me.
Forgiveness the central key
Its gentle way,
Holds the truth
Of our evolving universe.
Persistence works in faith
Equality for all time and place,
With certainty it is never weak.
All submits to Understanding
In the end anyway.
In this is our saving grace.

Every Hour

Every tree
Every flower
Every need
Every hour.
The land, the sea,
The air we breathe
Every child
Every seed,
All cared for
By the Mother.
All conditions
Guided by our deepest need,
To bring to earth
Full blossoming.

148

The Way

Trust is the soil
Upon which I stand
Stepping forward
On solid ground.
Through each travail
Strong and firm
With growing courage
I can not fail.
Faith is the flame
Held in my hands
A guiding light
To unknown lands.

Dear Grace

Please remove
Deceptions
From my mind
Fill my heart with Love sublime.
So I may see
With clarity
That only purity
Dwells in me.

Divine Mind

What could sweep away
All doubt and fear instantly,
But to realize the Supreme Mind.
Innocent and free
Held as pure and sweet,
Infinite in my true capacity
Made as God would have me be,
With joy of expanding this material creation.

What function in the pain we feel
What does it endeavor to reveal?
Deep within we must carry
Pain of some guilt
A judgement towards the creation
Resisting our own preciousness.
To then cast it out and reject
What we cannot accept
Upon the canvas of the world
Where we see the hidden play out.
But in the end this can not be
For Source creates perfectly.
We dwell for a time
In a little shell called "mine,"
And must own
These little fears along the way.
Pent up energy released as
More Divine is revealed,
Expansion is felt, inspiration comes.
All have shared
This bit of shame
So let us celebrate instead this day
This Source
From which we all came,
And choose forgiveness
In His Name.

Keep Smiling

We weep
Unable to see
The cause of human suffering.
We reach to control our destiny,
Half blind, our mind
Feels wrong inside.
A loving God would not condone
This endless carnage,
This paradox grinds us endlessly.
Seeking to crack the nut
That keeps us bound,
To understand what value our suffering might hold.
Could there be any sin
In the Divine heart of man?
Or did we lose our way somehow,
In ignorance choose limitation
For security or out of fear,
Did we set up little self as a God
Believing there is no heaven here?

We may be forced to yield
Brought to our knees
By adversity
We find simplicity revealed
A sense of certainty,
For nothing more can be lost
The slate wiped clean.
And yet we have prevailed
With old barriers gone, gives us relief.
Love truly conquers all
We take this lesson
Planting it deep,
Keep smiling
The nightmare is gone
This is the way
To inner happiness.

Companions

Hands of gratitude
Encircle my life,
Endless thanksgiving
My greatest wealth,
Lessons and learnings
Endless gifts,
Experience throws at my feet.
Of discourse between you and me
Spiraling open as a petal to light
My companions draw close
I hold them most dear,
To listen to the voice
Of Joy come near.
Safely I travel through every strife
Lifted by Spirit when clouds pass by.
I will tarry here awhile,
To accomplish my work
A sacred task, a promise once cast.
Forgiveness so close by my side
Until the end of all time,
I will realize my holiness
Acknowledge my true worth
As God's precious child,
For this I must come to truly embrace.
With Patience to carry me
In arms of great faith
Enveloped by the world
Held close to her breast
I feel her sacred Heart beating steadily
Giving me life.
Courage she counsels
Never doubt the result.
As Her only child
We can not fail the test.
With tender eyes I may appreciate
All as Love incarnate
Awakening to Divinity.

Crossroad

A choice
A diverging path,
Which one will bring me
The gifts that I seek?
A walking Sadhana
Without much foresight
Courage carries me forth,
With each breath
I dive deep.
Shall I follow my fear
And hesitate,
Do I yet know its face
Its stern countenance
And Death's false embrace?
Or can I choose strength and faith
Reliable friends
To soar to the heights
And tread instead a sure path of light?
A blissful sigh in with each step
Into life's full embrace,
I follow the road that
Uplifts my being.

Carefree

In thought, word and deed
We long to be free,
Stretching our backs
Arms flung wide as the sea
Falling backwards
In trust we will be held safely.
Oh, this is the Way
So many have sought
It must finally yield
A carefree fruit that fills our hearts,
Allowing Spirit within
To rule the day.

Gratitude

Caring for the self
Our brothers' and earth,
As if it were Heaven itself
As if we had accessed the full Source of life.
The Supreme fills our mind,
Inhabiting and enlivening every cell.
For as we give thanks
So simply, it seems
Filling up with gratitude
Our frequency quickens
Our bodies respond
We turn to the Sun to shine.
A balance of Nature
Once again can be found,
Here we are healed
Here life abounds
Here we master all within that we find.

Stillness

Embrace the stillness
Feel its power
Here is Peace
Guidance every hour.
Flow is easy
Little effort required
To move a mountain
To change our mind.
Cherishing each detail
The small reveals
Within a droplet
The sky.
A flower's scent
Holds Love's message
Our dear Mother deems is
Just what we need.
Hearts open as we draw in our breath
In Nature's perfumes
We merge again.

Filled with the essence of innocence,
A sweetness we feel
Resonates through every cell.

Union

Within the vows
Of union
A sacred trust is made.
Of love and fidelity,
To bind a man to his maid,
Or the honor of the state
Even unto the end of days
Each must be bound
By word and deed.
For even if we change
Our creed
We must in fact
Stand with some value
And inner integrity.

Tapestry

I am a tapestry
Spread upon a loom.
Dare I ask
For Whom do I weave
Or is the artist fully me?
I know I am both
Aligned with both
Weaver and loom.
When experience
Pulls in a color or thread
That is a contrast to what I expect
Is it fair to say
Some false note
Or error is made?
Perhaps, In the end
It will become the defining feature
I treasure most.

Cooperation

What is a life worth
What makes us strong
What nourishes our Soul all day long?
What is the point in this earthly game,
From which we care not to refrain?
Why is the remedy for humanity
So slow and hard
Why must we suffer our brother's blow,
What can the Supreme have in his heart
When our Spirit is born
Of his mind?
These ancient questions dog mankind,
But seem to me
Answered in some fall.
We lost awareness of who we truly are
By accident or hidden purpose
None can say
But an epic Quest
Haunts our history
To know what we believe is lost.
Yet this assumes a subliminal mind,
Not flesh but something more refined.
And through trials or conquest
The error is lost
And in great moments
We glimpse a grand design
A cloth whose
Wholeness escapes our mind.
Emulating at first
The Sage
With practice and discipline
Of our thought
Until the Master within is born,
Forged in fire
Purified in a cosmic wave,
Never again to believe this travail.

The Brightening

Each dawn
I open my eyes
Brightening my world
With an inner light.
I tune my speech
And acts, discrete
Towards the Highest Power
I may reach.
This is the work
As I putter around
That restores my Earth.
Her glory abounds
Filled with the heavenly
Sigh of the breeze
The little songs of birds at ease
And everything ascends in me.

Happy Self

Creating a happy countenance
A continuum of cheerful thoughts
Replacing all those little griefs
That plague one's inner harmony.
Nasty little shadow selves
Burrowing in my happy home,
For years and years they may remain
Hidden from my outer plane.
But once revealed the hunt begins
I send my legions to ferret them out
And turn them all around
So my Happy Self
Achieves Solidarity

Worthy of Love

Make a world
Where all Love may dwell
A golden place
Where all fear has been dispelled.
Permeate the atmosphere
With Wisdom and pure bliss
Every living thing here may now celebrate
Their own Divine Spirit.
Knowing they are worthy of Love
In each expression and every hue
All tones and qualities
Beloved by our Mother dear.

Fellow Man

I look
I listen
I allow,
With quiet mind
A gentle heart
To hear the echo
Of the Supreme.
His Offering,
Of all life now to me
And also to my fellow man.

Tropical Storms

Such storms prevail,
Squalls, flash floods
Swirling in the mind
Of every human soul.
Wreaking havoc
Breaking down
Old structures built on sand,
Murder, mayhem
Even righteousness.
Protecting our deepest fears
We cast them onto the stage of life.
In the dawn a simple fog
Dissolved by Sun's clear light.
Oh, when shall we realize
Our True Name
Fly free from our travail,
This endless wheel of violence towards the Self?
Each to see he is the incarnate
Of the Master of all Love,
Offering us at long last, the promised seed
We carry deep within our soul,
Of peace and harmony.
What do we really gain
From our wanton self-destructive strain?
Only now it seems to me
We struggle in this heartless game
So we may be washed repeatedly
Wave upon wave until not a drop of dark remains
Purified in every aspect,
Little by little or once for all
As Grace determines we should be.
Our task it seems,
At every turn,
Is choosing Love over fear,
Reaching out to our limit and
Up to the highest we may conceive
Becoming supple as a blade of grass
We learn to see the strength
Hidden beneath every weakness we perceive.

Moving Mountains

Undisturbed by appearance
Unmoved by distress
Undaunted by setback
Fluid as a stream.
With an optimism that fully comprehends
As children of the Supreme
We can not fail in our efforts.
If only we persist
We shall prevail in the end.

Creator's Love

As we love one another
To our deepest core,
The Creator's Love is this
And so much more.
His arms stretch beyond infinity
The Mother's heart expands throughout the world,
The Universe and
Realms Unknown.
They love their children
Even as we love ours
Without one drop of condemnation
For in Wisdom, all patterns find their place.
Just as our babe is not yet master of her capacity to walk
We know someday she will run and skip
We come to encourage her every step.
In this monumental task
And evolution's great work,
As one in our Source.
The only Child,
We are That
His name and mine
Are unified.
Here do I rest in the Mother's arms
Here do I suckle
And receive Her strength
To push on until the glorious day
When all Truth is revealed in me.
Here at last, even as expansion does not cease,
I will know with all
A well deserved
Everlasting Peace.

For Joy

Always it must be taught
And well-learned, it is advised,
That in the heart of weakness lies a hidden strength,
The purpose of the soul rests here.
All life revolves around this task.
To travel through a dark travail
Release the dragon coiled there
And set the power free.
By embracing it entirely
We achieve self-mastery.
From this we know our greatest joy
For this we soldier on
And in this we are not alone.

Blossoming

A friend once told me
A wonder of life,
Of cycles of rejuvenation.
The Gobi desert
Appeared devoid of life
Burst into a field of wild flowers.
After a 100 years of rest,
Of endless dust and drought
All seemed dead.
But as rains came
The ground swelled
Seeds had lain so still
No one imagined their hidden miracle,
Burst forth into radiant colors.
Once more casting their progeny
For a future promise
With a willing patience
For Grace to come and quicken them.

Great Strength

Flowing through life
With gentle ease
In the comfort of a God of Peace.
Reaching up to pluck
Ripened fruit
Of all we are here to do.
Stretching into harmony
Where all the aspects of my being
Come together to celebrate
A common goal,
With great vigor we travel home.
We are life inside a shell
But when timing makes us ripe
Our hidden splendor does appear
Spreading love upon the globe.
Our weakness but a shadowed veil
A blank shield
We wield until the time is right,
Revealing the great Strength
We hold inside.

My Guide

My Guide and dear friend
Sharing stories of rocks and seeds.
The constant renewal of all life
Each in our own way
And time,
A flowering as we intend to shine.
I feel assured
My mind at rest
My spirit raised to carry on.
Jotting down a recipe for a yummy drink
I receive the love she sends
It permeates my being.
A flower in the Mother's garden
I blossom now for her.

Inner Ease

I still hear small words of wisdom
That came to a child's ear.
The weight they held
Placing themselves
Easily in the inner pocket of my heart,
"Live and let live."
"To thine own self be true,"
"To each his own"
And the Golden Rule,
Lode stars in my life.
Admonitions to serve,
A simple wisdom in which to find,
Sweet inner ease,
To guide us safely through our lives.

Mastery

If I feel waves of sorrow
Washing over me,
Of loss or lack or any form
Of inner disharmony,
I know it is a call of soul
To pivot 180 degrees
To pierce a veil of inner fog
Weighing down on me.

To laugh, give thanks
Above each storm
Each weakness that I see,
All Suffering and travail,
Rests a power I possess
In some plane of my being.
I know to seek
As I take each step
To aim higher, dig deeper
For treasures just beyond my reach,
Hidden jewels waiting just for me.
Rare gifts,
In my journey of self-mastery.

Sweet Surrender

With sweet surrender
I find peace
My vision clears as I release
Control of my own destiny.
Still vaguely, I perceive
New steps unfold before me,
It is enough to take the risk
Carried forward by my faith.

Resentment is no key to happiness
Unlocking doors of sorrow,
As anyone must know.
Seeing miracles paves the way
To Heaven's grace,
In every face an opportunity,
Sent to guide me home.

Compassion knows the way with certainty,
She takes my hand joyfully
Showing me I the trick of it
As I let go into the Light
Carried to my Holy Grail,
A place of inner harmony.

Daily Task

Our daily tasks present a key
A blessing
Illumination and sacred seeds
Beneath a guise of infinite variety.
There is but one abiding theme
An ever repeating melody,
We are only light and frequency
Offering tones in a score.
Energy pouring into every pore.
In the play of life
It is not what or why
That matters most
But our rhythm of the acts
Holding our accord
Our offerings of Love,
As a flower unfolding
With gentle harmony
Enraptured by her beauty.
In Truth
Our own refrain
A gradual opening is felt,
All else a steady drone
Keeping pace
In the river of humanity,
Awakening to Grace.

My Pen

Dare I claim I am a voice for God
Yet with humble gratitude
Say also, so is every life,
As must be true
Nothing else is possible.
So, I take my pen
As boldly as a sword
To write a little prayer
For posterity.
Shine as brightly as the star
Ever twinkling in the firmament
Pulsing light upon our earth
Filling form with our dreams.
So gay with mirth
So giddy with joy
We flex our wings
And shoot straight home.

So do I dare to be so bold
To ask my God
Come forward now,
Accept me as I am
Whatever blemish I still retain.
Transform every cell
So I may know a Bliss that never wains
The jewel of my own true self,
And pour my cup
Upon this world.

Goodness

From the heart of Goodness
All life springs forth
Why can't we see this universal truth?
Clearly throughout the history of Man
Little progress has been found,
Perpetual suffering seems to dog our steps.
Still I imagine, as I carry on
This circumstance is will soon be gone.
A mask of impermanence,
For growth's sake,
An ever shifting sand
Stirs the waters
Where we find we are not bound
But free to cast our lines out into the great unknown.
We set the coarse,
Filled with obstacles to overcome
Our challenge revs us up.
New heights,
New vistas,
New frontiers
New places for self-mastery.
All held, somehow,
By a visceral fabric.
Love is Its
Unchanging ground
A firm foundation we may call upon,
From which worlds are born.

No Matter

No matter the challenges
That may lay ahead,
The remnants of suffering
Which cause my dread,
I cannot fail in the end.
For I am drawn by a Force
Greater than myself,
To realize I am more
Than the sum of my experience.
Not confined by thought
Or belief
Not the river of emotions
I may now feel,
Here my true Power lies
For me to more fully realize
The Mystery of the Universe
As it plays out in my little life.

Daily Prayer

Oh dear Mother
Of the universe
Mother of all mothers
I come to you,
Give to me
The Courage
The Faith
The harmonious perfection
As the instrument of Thy Peace.
Upon this body pour all love
Until every cell is full.
Help me transform
Expand beyond my farthest reach
My wildest dreams
With every step
To come to see
Stored freedom unleashed.
As I see what strings
Still hold me fast.
I cut the cords and only ask
In every thought, word or deed
Pure Self-honoring
Of my hidden Divinity.
I know you are my prayer,
And I spin like a top
To celebrate and give my gratitude,
Knowing wherever I feel weakness still
You help me build my inner strength.

Gentleness

Our sorrows may allow
Gentleness to expand
A Well deep and pure.
Healing waters of Compassion
Nourishing all life.
As we embrace our tender hearts
As a cherished gift
From which we never will depart.

My Belle

I do pray
Each day,
My thoughts and deeds
Align with Thee,
My Belle
And all You wish for me.
Please do not let me stray.
I rest here in my belief,
Trusting you know who I am.
From this place
I leap into the sky.
With every tiny jump
I hold my prayer
At my breast,
As my essential shield,
From uncertainty
I may feel.
Discovering I hold,
The Love
Who binds me to my soul.

Circle of Life

Wheels turn
Cycles unfold
Seasons pass
With best wishes for
New Years ahead.
We mark beginnings and ends
Picking up the threads
Committing ourselves to be
The changes we so long to see.
Changes in our lives
To honor the path
However unique
Without a hammer of judgment
Over all that we seek.
We make an effort,but never alone.
A sure road,
A mutual venture
In the Circle of Life,
Rests safely in our Great Mother's hands.
Knowing in our bones
We are equal
In value and capacity.
Spirit all.

Simple Joy

Why have we come
Who am I,
Perpetual questions
Of humanity.
Little extensions of the Divine
Our Mother's sweet and holy child.
We are on a mission so sublime,
To uncover the Godhead
In this hardest of stone
The rock of the physical
To which we are born,
A diamond of our Soul.
We bend our will and set the course,
To penetrate this hidden core
Of Life-force energy
Releasing the Infinite
From Its finite cage
For the simple Joy
Of our remembering.

My Best

Dear Spirit
Take up this life
And make of it
Your true Delight.
I try my best
As I am compelled by you
To make a structure
Fit for you.
But even this remains incomplete
Awaiting the quickening
I long from you to feel.

Clarion Bell

Oh hear this prayer
As I scratch out these words to Thee
That it be the highest
That may now flow through me.
To be the transformation
Of all I see
Pouring out as a simple
Thankfulness for all eternity.

To shine so bright
My twinkling little light
In the firmament of pulsing stars.
Upon our earth
Your master work
Filling hearts
So gay they roll in mirth.

So to be
As I would dream
To see at last who it is I came to be
Transformed into Thy clarion Bell
Ringing out in your great Symphony.

The Great Plan

Looking into the eyes
Of all I meet
I attempt to see
Through the veil of my mind,
To perceive the embodiment
Of the Supreme in all form.
Conjured up in His mind sublime
Birthed by the Great Mother
Squeezed Himself
Into this finite space
With all the trappings
Limitations bring.
And struggle out
As from a chrysalis
To conquer limitation itself.
We can not fail
For He is his Plan
Incarnated inside man.
We wander about
In a density
Feeling lost or alone
So identified with the skin we own.
But logic sheds a gleam
If all is God this can not truly be.
Still the earth of senses is as it seems
We must play this game
Of hide and seek,
But secretly we hold a growing faith
That we are in fact, guided by a steady hand
Standing beyond the Play
Whose methods may appear unclear to me.
Still we easily sense within,
Viewing Nature's majesty
Or in simple acts of generosity,
A plan for all life
Arriving home,
Full riches at once restored.

The Call

How shall I know
If I follow thee
Or do Thy Will?
How may I discern
Without Thy light
What measure can I use
To judge
What may be right?
You must come
Be my Guide
Take up the cause,
Then I may trust
I walk with Thee
And never tarry more
Where you can not be.
And be now the Light
You Will for me.

Behold Love's Face

Look deep into brother's eyes
Behold this face where Love dwells inside.
Perhaps hidden well
By some great disguise
Melting in Compassion's eyes.
Arise to see our world harmonize
Not perfect or of the purest light,
But easily transmuted by the what we share.
Each act of kindness
A spoken word,
The heart of Mercy
Sees our beauty stirred.
It is our own gentle nature
That we seek
Reflecting back in every face we see.

Unity

I stood my ground
Today
I found love
Anyway.
No matter our differences
They pale
In the greater Unity
We share.

1 6 6

Transmutation

I gather up threads of frustration
Any little dust of doubt
Sweep away my worries,
Dive into a river
Cool and clean and clear
Washing off all fear.
Gathering the reeds of old
Casting them one and all
Into the forge,
A transmuting Fire.
Its purifying flame
Turns all to Love again.
Out flows my true intent
Its healing golden ray,
Filling every part of me
With courage and deep tranquility
And helps me shine
As God would have me be.

Greatest Gift

I used to call them lessons
The challenges in life,
But now I realize their true quality
As my greatest Gifts.
I love them with all my heart
Even though I still might quake
And honor the doors
They carve in me
Dissolving all my fears.
Even if their process is a squeeze
I know to push through
To truly see.
I love these gifts that come to me
For practicing my gratitude,
For all the strength I gain
In my growing equanimity.

Tranquil Sea

Floating in a tranquil sea
Of love, light and inner harmony.
Arms stretched wide
Relaxed inside
I receive all blessings in my life.
My soul's purpose
And my destiny.

Help is Given

No need to push,
Pull or strain
I may relax
As the Presence within
Helps with everything.

True Power

In a flash of light
Truth welled up.
A child stands before a reflecting glass
Her image shining back
Looking into my eyes,
A strong conviction did arise.
A command arose in me,
"God is incapable of error
As his child, no mistake could be made."
From that day
I had my Ally.
No matter what hurt or how deep
My touchstone walked hand in mine.
I knew I could not truly fail
Unconditional Love is the true Power
I now knew inside.
If I stumbled,
Questioning my worth
He would help me rise.
I could carry on
No matter how long the road may be,
Perhaps for all eternity.

Not only my small story
But Evolution's principle.
All come to face their own unknown
With a growing confidence
To bring Love home,
To dance with Destiny,
No matter what our style.
In this Creation
Nothing is outside,
Earth nourishes each expression
And all will have their day,
Every form sustained
For True Power has the final say.

The Gift

We each carry
Within our being,
An infinite capacity.
The expression
Of our intention,
Plays out within our lives.
We wear a satchel
By our side
In which resides
A Dharmic treasury
An accounting of the love we feel.

The Creative Principle
Who knows not limitation.
By birthright, as expressions of this light,
In this alone place our trust.
That sharing of this Love
Fills us with all blessings,
Abundance flows
The Treasury can be expressed
In every aspect of our lives.
And our supply reflects the clear expression
Of our particular desires
All needs are met,
What we hold most dear decides the gift.

Song of the Soul

You are the Joy
That dwells in me
The abundance
The wholeness of my being.
You are the Grace
The harmony.
You are the sky
Clear and blue
The flowers blossoming
Green grasses too,
The wonderful shade trees
And little birds
Who fill my garden with song.
The friendships that cause my heart to fly
My Sun and Moon
And every wonder of this world
You are the everlasting Love
Of my life.
You are the
Song of the Soul.